I know the author
heart after God ar
have been lost to Jesus Christ and His Kingdom.

We have been in service with her many times and appreciate her spirit and dedication. We thank God that He brought her back from the dead to be with us, we hope, until Jesus comes.

—Pastor J. W. Copeland

Anita Shipman has written a book that will inspire and encourage you and let you know there is a better way and that life as we know it will be over very soon. She shows us how finding a rock can lead to a better life. How God can totally change a life and make it acceptable and ready to meet Jesus in the clouds of glory. As you read this book, we pray that you will allow Jesus to come into your heart and encourage you to be ready for the Lord's return.

—Reverend Larry Radach, evangelistic pastor

This book Anita wrote is from God. This book has a message to America, which is about His coming. This rock that the Lord gave to her is about His message that if you don't repent and receive Jesus, you will be left behind.

I pray that as you read this book, you will let the Holy Ghost open your spiritual eyes and heart to the truth that Jesus is coming soon.

—Sharron Church

Do you have loved ones who need salvation? Do you need a stirring up in the Gifts of the Holy Ghost? Would you like to read an amazing witness and testimony concerning the second coming of Jesus Christ? I highly recommend this book for everyone.

—*Stacey Ellis*

What an absolute amazing journey *The Rock* has taken us on as Anita explains to us the revelation of what God is showing her in the spirit. This is for the Kingdom of God, a tool to be used to reach the unreachable and encourage the saints who have been still. This is Anita's story but God's glory.

—*Pastor Curtis Leland*
First Baptist Church, Wagoner, Oklahoma

Anita's journey to heaven and back is one that takes on a profound message. She is an ordinary young girl that went through very difficult times. I enjoyed her transparent childlike description of her experience. You will feel like you were there. Anita is very dedicated to bringing the message that the Father sent her back with, and I am intrigued by how she is so sensitive to the Lord's leading.

She has a message and a tool that God has chosen to use in her life to shout to the world, "He is coming soon." You will be fascinated by her story and the miracles she has to share.

—*June Purnell*

Jesus is coming! And when you read this book, not only will it inspire you, but it will also give you hope until the return of the Lord.

I have known Anita Shipman during the time she suffered from her illness and after she was sent back from heaven with a message from the Lord about His coming. God has truly transformed her and blessed her with a rock that shows the revelation of His coming.

I pray that when you read this book, it will open up your spirit and pierce your heart so you will get your life right before Jesus returns for His children.

—Pastor Junior Mullin
Pentecostal Church of God, Pryor, Oklahoma

GOD'S *Gift*

GOD'S *Gift*

THE ROCK

Anita J. Shipman

TATE PUBLISHING
AND **ENTERPRISES**, LLC

Published by Tate Publishing & Enterprises, LLC
127 E. Trade Center Terrace | Mustang, Oklahoma 73064 USA
1.888.361.9473 | www.tatepublishing.com

Tate Publishing is committed to excellence in the publishing industry. The company reflects the philosophy established by the founders, based on Psalm 68:11,
"The Lord gave the word and great was the company of those who published it."

Book design copyright © 2014 by Tate Publishing, LLC. All rights reserved.
Cover design by Harold Jason Branzuela
Interior design by Mary Jean Archival

Published in the United States of America

ISBN: 978-1-63268-089-1
Religion / Christian Ministry / Preaching
14.08.20

Contents

My Testimony: The Illness Only God Could Cure

Before this book is read, I would like to say thank you to the ones who made this book possible for me: God, Jesus Christ, and the Holy Ghost. This book would have never been possible if it wasn't for God saving me with His grace and mercy. I am thankful that we have a forgiving and loving God because I would not be here today if it wasn't for God's grace and mercy and His Son, Jesus Christ, who died on the cross so I could be forgiven for my sins. I love you, God, Jesus, and the Holy Ghost. Thank you for loving me and giving me this opportunity to write this book and deliver the message of the Rock to America that explains the coming of Jesus Christ.

I could start this book in so many different ways because my life has gone in so many different directions. My name is Anita J. Shipman (Frakes). I was born on March 23, 1981, to

Lala D. Frakes (Swift) and Steven A. Frakes in Bartlesville, Oklahoma. I have been married to my loving husband since 2005, but we have been together since kids in high school. Together we're blessed to have two wonderful children to share our lives with.

My husband and I work at the family funeral business in Oklahoma. It's very ironic that someone with a life-threatening and an unknown illness with chronic pain had the responsibility of helping lay to rest many of God's children before they made their final transition to the grave and beyond. I didn't know it then, but I was going to have a life that was full of adventure, heartache, lies, misunderstandings, pain, and worries. But one thing is certain: the journey was so worth it.

I mentioned earlier that I was born in the spring of 1981. The question is when did I die? As a little girl, I had episodes or spells, where I would get extremely dizzy and be subject to lying in bed for hours on end with the dry heaves. Of course this resulted in a concerned family seeking answers that just weren't there. Maybe something just threw my equilibrium off from time to time. But that was just a symptom of the first unexplained sickness of many more to come throughout different periods of my life.

I would continue to have dizzy spells for years until the age of twenty-four, when, thankfully, they subsided. By this time, I was making preparations to marry my soul mate. We had just announced our wedding plans, and two weeks, later we found that I was expecting our first miracle.

But before this little treasure was born, we were united in marriage by a true angel of God, Reverend Virgil Limb, who was also lovingly known as Gene in the small community we live in. I will tell you now that I am truly blessed to have had Gene and my husband in my life, along with everyone that I mention here. I came to realize, whether in good or bad circumstances, without the individuals I met and the relationships we created, I honestly feel that I wouldn't be here today. And it's all because each person was a necessary part of my life and somehow helped me make it through this incredible journey God has planned for me.

My six-year journey of an unknown illness that caused a lot of pain and unexplainable symptoms began after the birth of our son, Ryan. When Ryan was delivered, we realized right away that he was a big boy. He weighed ten pounds and six ounces; measuring twenty-two and three-quarter inches long, he was big. He obviously had nowhere to go, so he had his feet up in the very top of the right side of my rib cage, and when he would kick, you could see his elbows stick out and his feet move when he would squirm around. Anyone who has been pregnant or has been with someone who was knows what I'm talking about.

Ryan was delivered C-section by the doctor, and I was put under anesthesia while he finalized the operation. After surgery, I was returned to my room, and I remember being jarred as the nurses placed me from the surgery bed to my hospital bed in the maternity ward. This was very painful and caused me to raise this question: could that particular moment have contributed to my illness? I truly don't think so.

About two hours after our son was born, my husband and I were notified by a nurse that our son had tested positive for a bacterial infection and they were going to keep him in the nursery, administer some antibiotics, and keep a watchful eye on him. I should have paid attention a little closer.

So our son was treated with several rounds of antibiotics and kept from us for hours while he was being treated for the infection. Sometime later, we were released and sent home, and I seemed to be doing just fine. Once home and settled in, my husband and I went to bed excited with the new life that we had created, and we were looking forward to sharing our lives with this new bundle of joy.

The morning after we brought our son home, I woke up with the most horrible pain in my abdomen, worse than labor pains. I had gone through ten hours of labor with no pain medicine until it was time for the C-section, so I knew this was not normal, and my body was telling me something was wrong.

I called my husband and told him something wasn't right, so he came home, picked me up, and took me back to the doctor's office. But the doctor who delivered our son was out of the office that day, and I was seen by the doctor who was on call. He did an examination and reassured us that these were normal pains after having a C-section. The doctor suggested a different type of pain medicine to see if it would help relieve the symptoms. So after returning home, I adjusted the medicine regimen, but the pain continued. I noticed that every time I would eat something, the pain would flare up and my abdomen would begin to swell on the right side of my rib cage. I had never experienced this type of pain before. The only way I could get relief was by lying down.

After changing my diet regimen, the pain continued and began to get worse, so I began my personal journey seeking a physician who could help me understand what was wrong. I began to see doctor after doctor, each having a new perspective, which led to the removal of my gallbladder early into the first year. The operation was done by the most honest and remarkable doctor that I ever met in my life. My gallbladder was removed and tested negative, although the medicine from all the tests caused my body to react in a way indicating that the organ was indeed in poor condition.

But even though the tests produced negative results, the doctors and technicians noticed I had a swollen spot near the right lower intercostal region of my rib cage. *The gallbladder was removed, and the surgeon noted that the gallbladder looked unremarkable, but findings after surgery revealed some edema around the posterior wall of the gallbladder.*

After the gallbladder was removed, I continued to suffer from pain and swelling on the right side of my abdomen. I was sent to a chiropractor to see if maybe I just possibly had a rib out of place, which might have occurred during the delivery of our son, that was inflicting the pain. But the pain only continued and was getting worse as time went by.

In April of 2007, we discovered our family of three was going to be a family of four. So I stopped taking the medicine I was on that helped control the symptoms and pain of the illness I was suffering from. But what I didn't realize was that the illness I was suffering from was going to affect our baby that I was carrying and cause her pain like I was suffering from.

I noticed that after I became pregnant with Addison, our daughter, that the symptoms and pain that I had been suffering from had subsided. But once Addison was born, the symptoms and pain I had encountered before she was conceived came back with a vengeance. It was really bizarre. My pregnancy with Addison was much more difficult than the one I had with our son, Ryan. From the very beginning, it felt as though she was fighting to get out of the womb. I began to have contractions early on in my pregnancy, which resulted in several phone calls to the doctor, but he reassured me that everything was just fine and, more than likely, I was just dehydrated. So I took the doctor's advice and drank plenty of water and rested as much as I could. I had finally hit the last trimester of my pregnancy and began going to the doctor on a weekly basis. It was two weeks before Addison was scheduled to be delivered that we went to our weekly appointment and received some startling news.

It all began with the nurse taking my blood pressure. She noticed it was high, and she asked if I was stressed or having any pain. I told her yes, I had been having contractions on a regular basis. The nurse called my doctor into the room. After the doctor examined me, he looked at my husband and me with this concerned look on his face and told us he wanted to put me on a monitor to see how the baby was doing. I was connected to the monitor for a while when the doctor came in, removed a portion of the printed test results, and, after a short pause, said, "I need you to go straight over to the hospital and get checked in. We need to deliver your baby now! If she kicks one more time, she could rupture open your old C-section scar and you both will be in danger."

My husband and I didn't have anything with us to bring our new little girl home in, let alone a change of clothes for me. I asked the doctor if we could drive back to our house and get the overnight bags I packed for us, and he replied, "No, I'm sorry, you don't have time."

In less than an hour, we went from having one child to two. Addison Nicole was born on November 10, 2008, and her life started out very painful. I remember the next morning, when my husband called me from home and asked me, "How's my little baby girl?"

I replied, "She's a hold-me baby."

He jokingly said that I was spoiling her. So I let him know one can't spoil a baby who's not even a day old. She would be released from the hospital with a clean bill of health.

Let me tell you, just because they release your child from the hospital with a clean bill of health doesn't mean they are healthy. Addison was a very sick baby. I knew deep within my soul that colic was not the reason for her discomfort. It was only an excuse. So what was the problem? I still wouldn't know until I found salvation through our Lord God. I would have to hold Addison day and night, rocking her in my arms from one end of the hallway to the next for the first two months of her life. When I would lay her down to change her diaper, she would stop breathing until her little lips would almost turn blue. So what was wrong with her? How did she get so sick when I was pregnant with her?

We went to three doctors in the first two months of Addison's life. The first doctor gave her medicine that caused seizures and other side effects. The second doctor gave her another type of medicine, which had no effect. The third gave her two shots and sent her home with three prescriptions. He told us she had colic. "Just hang in there, and it will end in about six months."

Not knowing any different, I did just what the doctor told me to do (I knew if I had to wait six months for this hurt baby to quit crying, I was going to lose my motherly nerves). The day came when I had finally reached my wit's end with the nonstop walking, bouncing, and crying.

I gently laid Addison down on her back on a blanket I had placed on my living room floor. I pushed on the front side of her little body from head to toe, and she never cried or made a sound. I then realized whatever was bothering her was not on the front side of her body, so I rolled her over on her tummy and pressed on her back. When I touched the right side of her back, just under her shoulder blade, she screamed just like she had been doing for months on end. I was so frightened about what just happened that I called my husband's parents. They came to our house right away, and his mom sat down on the floor, holding my baby girl. My father-in-law gently put his hand on Addison's back and rubbed downward. As he was doing that, he felt something move and pop exactly in the spot where I pressed on her when I had her on the floor.

I wondered what in heaven's creation was happening. After that, Addison never once cried again until the next evening, when she was held and passed around by some of our friends.

Of course I was excited to tell the doctor that we had finally figured out what was wrong with our baby girl. So we were at the doctor's office, and I wanted to let him know that we believe she has something out of place, and that was why she was crying; it only made sense. I explained to the doctor what happened, and he basically looked at me and might as well have told me I was crazy and didn't know what I was talking about. And, of course, without any notice to my husband, I proceeded to let the physician know that he basically wasn't listening to what I was trying to tell him, and I refuse to give my little girl any more of his prescribed medicine.

My husband and I made it home after a long ride in the car with a crying baby, because it hurt her to be buckled into a car seat. Desperate for an answer, when I returned home, I did what every physician tells you not to do, which is research to find a cure on my own. I got on the internet, e-mailed five osteopathic doctors, and told them what was going on with our little girl.

Out of those five, only one answered. She made us an appointment right away without hesitation. When we arrived at her office, she put her hands on my baby and discovered our little girl had two ribs out of place. Addison's right upper thoracic cavity was compressed and her right hip was out of place. After hands-on treatment, we left that office, and our little girl never cried again with the pain she had during the previous months.

When I was pregnant with Addison, I would always comment, "It feels like she is fighting to get out." My body was having contractions, and with her body position, those contractions pressed down on Addison, which caused the misalignment in her ribs and hip, and caused her to have a compressed upper thoracic cavity.

Looking back, I know that if I wouldn't have paid attention to the fact that when I would lay her down she would stop breathing after a few minutes, she probably would have died. Her cause of death would most likely have been certified as sudden infant death syndrome (SIDS). It's my opinion that SIDS and colic have something in common. Both are in a generic classification of an unexplained or, better yet, unexplored phenomenon. But yet the physician who had Addison's life in his hands two days before that just wanted to give her more medicine and diagnosed her with colic. I believe now that we have got to stop and listen to our own bodies and the bodies of our children and take into account all of the factors before we rush to the doctor's office. This will better the chances of the doctor being able to determine a proper diagnosis. Certain medicines can often times camouflage the symptoms we are having, so this is why it's so important to stop and listen to what our bodies and the Holy Ghost is telling us. A thorough explanation to your physician will only better the odds of him or her to accurately treat the condition.

After our daughter was born, my health began to worsen, so I went to my local doctor in town, and he tried very hard to get me answers. He ran multiple blood tests and performed numerous physical examinations, trying everything he knew possible to relieve the pain I was suffering from. Often there were times he was stumped and looked at me like I was crazy because you could see the swelling and symptoms that this illness caused, but no test could detect it. Around this time, I had been treated for an autoimmune disease.

Addison would end up getting better after seeing the osteopathic doctor in Tulsa, but she still wasn't 100 percent healthy, and I still wasn't paying attention closely enough. When she reached the age of two, Addison was sent home from her day care with high fever, abdominal bloating, diarrhea, pain, and she began to pass blood in her stool and would lose control of her bowels. It was shortly after we had returned home from a vacation that the symptoms of this illness hit her. It lasted for a month and put us traveling to her pediatrician's office three to four times a week, seeking treatment.

In the beginning, the doctor couldn't figure out what was causing the high fever and the other symptoms through standard testing, so he told Jason and me it would be okay to send Addison back to day care, so we did. The following day, her nurse called us at work and asked where our daughter was, and we responded, "She's at day care, why?" She responded saying Addison was highly contagious and we should immediately go to the day care and pick her up and take her to the doctor's office for treatment. She also told me that the stool sample that was taken and that after a long incubation period, the results showed Addison had a highly contagious bacterium called *Shigella sonnei D.*

The nurse told me that *Shigella* is a bacterium that affects the digestive track, resulting in symptoms that include diarrhea, cramping, vomiting, and nausea, which lead to more serious complications and possible death. The infection will sometimes cease on its own, but antibiotics might shorten the severity and duration of the illness. The bacterium produces toxins that attack the lining of the large intestine, causing swelling, ulcers on the intestinal wall, and bloody diarrhea.

I asked how this bacterium is transmitted. The nurse explained that the bacterium is transmitted through fecal matter, and they were required to report her infection to state health officials.

The following day, I was contacted by our local health department. They wanted to know in full detail where we had been with our daughter the past few days. We were told to keep her away from the general public until she had produced consecutive stool samples that were confirmed negative. Considering the incubation period, this is a very slow process. Now looking back, that was a sign from God to help me figure out what was wrong with me, but I still wasn't listening. Remember, I am not licensed to practice medicine. All I know is what was revealed to me through the Holy Ghost after being healed and saved by God's grace and mercy.

If I got sick after the birth of our son and my body was already being poisoned then, what happened when I was pregnant with our daughter? Was she being poisoned from my body? When I became pregnant with Addison, I never experienced the symptoms I was having before I became pregnant with her, but after she was born, everything came back. I was unknowingly sharing the toxins with our unborn child. It wasn't until the age of two that the bacteria started attacking her body like it was mine. I praise God that He led us to a pediatrician who had the wisdom and knowledge to figure out Addison's illness; otherwise, the situation would have ended up much differently. The doctor treated her with several rounds of strong antibiotic shots in her legs before her body was able to overcome the bacteria. I believe God was trying to show my husband and me what I was also suffering with, but I wasn't listening.

Sometimes some of the important symptoms are the most embarrassing, but if you are meeting with one of God's true angels, they won't find it embarrassing or humiliating at all. We as patients have got to be more open about our symptoms. If I would have been more open about my own, I now know the doctors would have figured it out. No one should ever have to experience what I experienced, but on the other hand, I would not change one thing I did in those six years. I did what God had set out for me to do, and I believe He has a bigger plan for me now that doesn't include all of the pain and misery.

Never Think God Is Not with Us Just Because We Don't See Him

I finally felt, as a mother, I had settled that unsettling feeling in me that something else was wrong with our daughter. By the time Addison was two, I had become very ill I had to take multiple prescriptions and rely on narcotics to help relieve my pain. For years, I went somewhere once a week to get a massage. My husband sometimes commented, "Why do you continue to go and get a massage when you seem to feel bad for a week after that?"

Technically, it wasn't the masseuse's fault. Each massage felt wonderful. My body would relax, and the aches and pains seemed to slowly disappear. At least for a few hours I was able to have some relief. However, I believe the reason I would continue to be sick is because along with each massage, the gentle and sometimes deep-tissue rub was causing the infected lymph nodes to release their stored toxins, releasing the poison throughout my body and causing it to spread further into my system.

Leading up to the time that I was healed and saved by God, my symptoms were only getting much worse. By this time, I had been to several different doctors and had been through numerous tests and examinations.

I would have lymph nodes removed from my right groin that showed signs of infection and possible cancer but tested negative. I had my tonsils removed, laparoscopic surgeries performed, and numerous other operations, where no cure was to be found. I had been treated for an autoimmune disease, fibromyalgia, Parkinson's disease, hepatitis A, and several other conditions. At the end of my journey, I was seen by Dr. Debra Madaj, who worked countless hours with my husband and me trying to figure out what was making me so sick. She ran multiple blood tests, MRIs, scans, and nerve tests, but when we received no answers from all the tests, she recommended sending me to the Mayo Clinic in Rochester, Minnesota. Dr. Madaj had decided that I might be suffering from a rare type of nerve disorder that caused all the bizarre symptoms that I was having.

I knew this was my one last hope. I could already feel my body beginning to shut down from all the pain and everything it had been through. I remember thinking as the date got closer, *How are we going to afford this?* But I was not bothered by it like I normally would have. I knew from a feeling I had inside of me that the end of my own personal hell was going to be over before I could ever make it to Minnesota. When I went to bed at night, I would pray, "Lord, please forgive me of my sins now because if you are real, I don't want to confess them in front of you." I never really knew if God, Jesus, or the Holy Ghost was real. But God knew all along what He had planned for me and how He was going to prove to me and my family that He, indeed, is real.

Even knowing what financial burden my husband and I were soon to be facing, I wanted to go on one last trip with our children. I truly believed that I would die before ever making it to the Mayo Clinic. For some reason, I had a strong desire to get away with my husband and kids before I was sent to the Mayo Clinic for several weeks. Because of my condition, I knew we would have to stay close to home, so we chose Eureka Springs and Branson, Missouri. Eureka was not part of the plan at first. But on the day before we were supposed to leave for Missouri, I had a hunch to leave that evening when Jason got home from work. I didn't know why, but I just had a feeling that we needed to leave one day earlier than scheduled.

Our first destination would take us to the Basin Park Hotel in Eureka Springs, Arkansas. We arrived around 10:45 p.m. The next morning, after breakfast, we did some sightseeing and then got back on the road and headed to our second destination, Roaring River State Park in Cassville, Missouri. We were only staying there for one night, so we wanted to arrive early to let the kids enjoy the trout fishing and the beautiful scenery.

We arrived at our cabin around 11:00 a.m., which was too early to check in, so we walked around the banks of the river and let the kids play and fish. It was soon time to check in, so we located our cabin, which happened to be on the side of a mountain that included three separate sets of stairs. Climbing stairs was a horrible thing for me to do with the condition my body was in. I looked at my husband and said, "Why don't we just take a change of clothes out of our luggage instead of carrying all of it up these stairs?" He never argued with that idea. Unknowingly, I found that this was going to be a very defining day in my life. After all the activity I had from our trip, I had become tired and wasn't feeling very well. It was around 3:00 p.m. and the kids started getting hungry, so my husband drove us to the adjoining town about seven and half miles away.

As we were going into town, I noticed that I was feeling much different than I had felt before. I became extremely weak and could feel myself fading in and out of conversations, and nothing made any sense to me. Then I noticed my vision had changed. I no longer could make out buildings or where I was. Everything was black. I could still hear my husband and children talking as I started going down this dark tunnel; it was as though they wouldn't let me go. But then the voices disappeared. I couldn't see or hear anything for a long time. Everything was just black.

The next thing I remember is being laid down in a bed, and I said, "I love you, and I'm sorry," and was given a kiss on my forehead. And they said, "It's going to be okay." The room was real bright. It was a light like I had never seen before. Then the person who laid me down just walked out of the room. Until I was able to remember what had happened on this particular day, I just assumed that my loving husband had carried me up the three flights of stairs to our cabin and laid me down in bed and I was talking to him. I knew that I didn't walk up the stairs because I remembered being carried and laid down in bed, and I remembered that the person who had laid me down was wearing a beautiful white gown. But when I started recanting the story to my husband the following morning, he told me that he did not carry me up the stairs and that he actually had to make two trips to the cabin. One trip was to carry our daughter, who was asleep in the car, up the stairs and a second trip to carry the food because I was incoherent, and he had to bring me back to the cabin before they were able to finish their dinner. Then he made a comment that made everything all too real. That comment made me realize exactly when I died and at what point I crossed over, only to return with a plan from God.

My husband said to me in the car on the way back to the cabin, "You said 'I love you, and I'm sorry.' You were crying and mumbling the words." He then went on to say that I was the first one out of the car and up the stairs and into the bedroom. When he checked on me after getting everyone settled, he recalled I was sweaty, pale, and looked like I was in a deep sleep. It was a sleep that changed my life forever. And so the question to ask is if that wasn't my husband I saw and talked to or who kissed me and said, "It's going to be okay," then who was it? It was my angel. As my physical body was lying in bed in our cabin, my soul and spirit was traveling to a place I never knew existed. Because I was not saved, I didn't go straight to heaven. I was shown things that I never could have imagined existed.

I woke up at ten o'clock the next morning. I remembered feeling amazed that I was even alive. I was nauseated, dehydrated, and felt a little weak, but by the grace of God, I had packed the bottle with just that one pill for nausea, so I took it. Not knowing yet what had happened the previous evening, I never acknowledged or was aware of what I had been through. My family and I packed all our stuff and headed to our third destination. We would end up changing resorts four times before returning home from our trip. We made it to Chateau on the Lake in Branson, Missouri, and because the rooms were so expensive, we only were able to stay one night. We decided to just hang out at the hotel pool for the day, get up the next morning, and go to the beach that we could see from our balcony. All I really remember from that part of the trip was the pool and how the staff carried around cold towels for their guests to enjoy on a hot summer day. But now looking back, I knew I was already feeling better, or I would have never been out in the sun by the pool in the heat of July for hours.

The next day, we headed over to the beach that we viewed from our balcony the previous day. We got all our chairs, canopy, food, ice chest, and the kids' toys carried down to the beach and set up. This is the day that I began to notice that something about me had changed. I didn't know what yet, but I knew I wasn't experiencing the pain or weakness I had been for years. As we were sitting there, watching our children play, we noticed there was a group of people doing a baptism. It wasn't just a simple service by any means. It took them a couple of hours to complete the prep work and to get everyone ready.

As I was sitting there, enjoying watching my children swim, I began to watch the ritual that was taking place in front of me. At one point, they were baptizing a girl, and my son was swimming right in the middle of them. I thought, *Oh no!* But then I thought to myself how brave these people are to be doing this type of ceremony right in front of nearly two hundred people. So I watched as they baptized three girls and one man, all wearing white garments. One by one, they were taken into the water and baptized. They chanted as they were entering and leaving the water, and it was an amazing sight. After the baptism ritual ended, everyone in their group was gathered to take a picture, so I decided to go up and offer to take the picture for them so no one was left out.

About a half hour later, I started to feel some discomfort. I asked my husband if we could start heading toward our final destination and get checked in so I could lie down and rest. But little did I know I didn't at all need to lie down and rest that day. God had taken those days away from me, and He was getting ready to prove it to me. When my husband and I pulled up to the Welk Resort in Missouri, which was about fifteen minutes away from the beach, my husband got out of the car and went inside to the front office to check in and get our room key. When he returned to the car, I said with a tone in my voice, "Please get me to our room. I have got to go to the bathroom."

After we arrived where our room was located, I jumped out of our car, went to the hotel room, unlocked the door, and found the bathroom. I remember feeling a lot of pressure like you do when you're about to deliver a baby. I sat down on the potty, placed my hand on the silver bar that they provide for the handicapped, and closed my eyes. When I got up and opened my eyes and I went to flush the stool, I remember thinking to myself, *That looks like blood. I should probably tell Jason so he can tell the doctors.* But then I heard a voice say, "Why, they won't know what it's from."

Within a matter of minutes, all the swelling I had in my abdomen disappeared, and I lost fifteen pounds. I not only had finally passed the blockage that was stuck in my large intestine but also had excreted large doses of the bacteria from a ruptured abscess that had been inside my intestine for the past six years. Not once have I been sick with the "unknown illness" I suffered from for six years, nor have I even been back to see a doctor since that day. It took me a while for my body to get rid of the poisoning on its own, but it happened, and I owe it all to the power of God.

Do I believe I am healed? Absolutely, without a shadow of a doubt, and I owe this to God and His angels that surround me every day. I praise God every day for the gift of healing. For six years, my body was being slowly poisoned after the birth of our son, and when I got pregnant with our daughter, she as well received a continual dose of that same poison, and she was never treated until she was two years old. How do I know this? Because I died and went to heaven. God healed and saved me, and when I was baptized with the Holy Ghost, I received the knowledge and wisdom to figure out what my illness truly was.

Never Underestimate the Power of God

We left from our vacation one day earlier than we had planned and headed back home. I wasn't hurting or feeling bad. I was just excited to come home. I could tell there was something different about me. I now believe that several transitions exist in our lives when we are saved and become a born-again child of God. I know I still have other transitions to come in my life. Every day is always a new day for me. I have struggles and new learning experiences each day. I now know that it is part of being a child of God, and giving no place to the devil but instead to listen to God and let Him know what you are struggling with. And, if you will listen, you will hear Him and understand.

I believe if we just pay a little closer attention and listen to what God and the Holy Ghost are telling us, and guiding us to do, we will have a joyful and fulfilling life here on earth. It's so simple. Just pray, listen, and be obedient to God, and do what He asks you to do, even if you have to do it alone.

As for the etiology to my unknown illness, please remember I do not have a license to practice medicine. God revealed to me what made me sick for six years and what I had died from. After I was baptized in the Holy Ghost, I worked many hours researching my medical records and putting the pieces together with the wisdom and knowledge that I received as a blessing from God.

I was a healthy twenty-four-year-old woman when I became pregnant with our son, so I knew that my illness had to begin either while I was pregnant with him or shortly thereafter. During my pregnancy with Ryan, everything went great. Not once did I ever become sick or have any complications. It was a picture-perfect pregnancy. So at what point did the illness begin?

After hours of labor, the doctor decided that he would need to deliver Ryan by C-section. During the entire pregnancy, Ryan always stayed on the right-hand side of my body in my rib cage. As the doctor was delivering him, he had to do a lot of pulling and tugging to get Ryan out, and during this process, my large intestine became torn, which caused a lesion. When bacteria within the intestinal tract came in contact with the lesion, it caused an abscess to grow on the inside of my intestine. Slowly, as the abscess grew, my body was being poisoned. As the abscess grew larger, my intestinal blockage became much greater, which added additional bacterial poisoning. But before any severe blockage had occurred, our daughter was conceived. When that happened, she would take part of the poison, and my symptoms would subside.

But after she was born, the symptoms came back and hit me like a ton of bricks. I began to have cysts that would form in my breasts and showed all the signs of breast cancer but were tested negative. I had cysts in my legs that doctors could see with their eyes, but when they ordered a test, nothing abnormal would show up. I now know these were little sacks of poison that would build up because my lymph nodes couldn't filter the poison fast enough. I experienced night sweats that were so severe that I would have to get up in the middle of the night and change my bedding and clothes. There were nights I would walk the floor for hours trying to find relief from the pain, but not even some of the strongest narcotics could control it. I had unexplainable weight gain and fever.

After my last surgery in November of 2011, I had lymph nodes that showed physical signs of cancer removed from my right groin, but the test results would show no answers. Then one month after my lymph node removal, I developed an infection at the surgery point. So why did my lymph nodes look as though they had cancer? Because they were infected with the bacteria that my body was poisoned with, and they could no longer filter the poison. They were worn out. Our lymph nodes are designed to filter the poisons in our body, and when our body is overloaded with bacteria and poison, they stop working properly.

Why did my back hurt and my legs and arms have numbness? It wasn't that I had anything out of place or a nerve disorder. I just had a lot of swelling from the abscess in my large intestine, and the poison in my body affected my nervous system. When that happened, the intestinal pressure pushed on the nerves that affected my legs and arms. At one point of my journey, I began to have little cysts form in my sinus cavity, which caused the blackouts and the spells of being incoherent. That's why I would wake up with blood on my pillow, which was also unexplainable to doctors.

After six years of pain and countless doctor visits and tests, not one person could figure out what was wrong with me, except God. If I would have known then what I know now about the powerful healing God performs on people, I would have sought God and attended church. But I was searching for man to heal me and for a machine to give me a diagnosis. Although this was a hard lesson to learn, I know God is showing me now that this is exactly why America is in danger of Christ's return, because we are turning to man for everything and not turning to God for what we need.

I have met many people during the six years I was sick. When I died and was returned back to earth, I was given the knowledge to see why I was sick and figure out things that most people couldn't. The Lord opened my ears and helped me pay attention to His voice. I was suddenly blessed; I'm still being blessed and will continue to be until my journey here on earth is complete, because I have made a vow to God and I'm not going to turn around now. When I was sick, I was always scared to die. It wasn't that I didn't want to die alone, but I was scared of being left alone once I did die. I didn't know where I was going to be.

Like many people today, I never knew if God was real, if Jesus was real, or if heaven and hell really existed, but now I know the truth. Now I am excited, not to die but to tell people about the powerful Gospel of Jesus Christ and how God is still sitting on the throne today, waiting to send His only Son, Jesus Christ to come back and get us. I know the day I take that one last step, which completes the plan God has for me, I'll go home and become a part of a beautiful celebration in heaven.

I am blessed to be healthy, happy, and joyful and still have family and friends by my side after the past six years of my life. It has not been easy. I have had to go back to the people I hurt while I was sick and say, "I'm sorry, please forgive me." I knew I hurt them, but I also knew I needed them in my life at that time, and still do today. We have all made mistakes; that's why we have a God that forgives and loves each one of us.

God truly blessed me when He gave me my husband. He is a strong man who would always push me whenever I didn't want to go any further. They both were always there no matter the time, circumstance, distance, or cost. God and Jason were the two persons in my life who never gave up on me. And for that I am thankful. It takes a lot of faith, strength, and love to help your spouse and to be there for them when they are sick, and I praise God every day for giving me such a loving and strong husband.

If You Believe in God,
He Will Believe in You

You may ask how I know that there are different transitions that take place. This is because on April 26, 2012, when I was so sick and felt that I would soon die, I sat down and wrote a letter to my husband, son, and daughter. Each letter was special and contained things I wanted each of them to remember me by. I also wrote a description of what I wanted at my funeral service after I died. It was a complete, full-detailed account of what music I wanted my husband to play at my funeral. I placed everything in a metal filing box and gave it to my father-in-law so he would make sure my husband got what I wanted him to have. The service was planned out just as I wanted it. Every detail was considered and covered so it would be a memorable time for those left behind to cherish. Nobody could tell the story like I could.

I really thought this was God's way of helping me find my way in a new journey. But He was answering many of the questions He knew I would have after He healed me and sent me back from heaven. In the back of the book, I have included the letters I wrote to my family that day. I ask forgiveness for the mistakes that are present in the notes to my family. But all things considered, I wasn't worried about grammar at the time. The original notes are so important to me that I couldn't consider making corrections.

So why do these letters tell me that we have many transitions after our rebirth as a Christian? Because I never knew I was coming back, and I sure didn't know when I signed off on my husband's letter there was more to come. Nor did I know that when I wrote "I will be your Sparkling Angel from above" that meant I would have the most gorgeous sparkle in my eyes when I returned from above, and that, yes, my kids would get hurt because they did lose their mom whom they once knew, just like my husband lost his first wife that day on July 19, 2012. I know now that was God talking through me in those letters, and He knew they would help after being completely changed from the person I used to be.

God has completely changed me from who I used to be. Before I was healed and shown a glimpse of heaven, I hadn't once ever read the Bible and would very seldom attend church. I had a soul that was headed straight to hell. I hoped that God was real, but like a lot of people today, I wasn't sure. During my illness, I worked every day. I began working at our office in Wagoner, Oklahoma, when Addison was a baby. When God sent me back from heaven, I had to relearn everything that I once knew. It was as though He completely wiped away my memory of everything I had experienced in those six years. I had to relearn what I did at work, my husband, and my kids—everything was absolutely new. I had been reborn into a healthy body. I even had to relearn time. In heaven, it's as though there's no essence of time, unlike here on earth. I believe a lot of people in America underestimate the power of God. I wasn't healed by man but by God and saved with His grace and mercy.

Our Angels Are with Us

As I go through the transitions in my life, I find more answers by praying and seeking God and listening to what He is telling me through the Holy Ghost. I truly believe I will go through different transitions until I enter heaven again. I have heard several stories about other people who have gone to heaven ever since my experience. I have also heard people's testimonies about going to hell and the Lord showing them that hell is real. It's important for us to talk and share those stories more often with the people around us. One of the reasons some people don't believe in God is because we don't take the opportunity to share our testimonies with each other. Most of us just push it to the side. We have got to share God's Word and let others know He is real and He is here with us every single day.

When I returned back home from our vacation after my trip to heaven and my healing took place, one thing I was still relying on was my pain medicine. It wasn't that I hurt; it was that it had become a habit after being on them for six years. Then one day, God got a hold of me. I was at work and decided that I would take one of my pain pills, so I asked my husband for one. After I took the pill, I felt the most overwhelming feeling of guilt, like I had done something to upset someone. One thing you must understand is that I am sometimes very hard headed and ornery. So the next day, I asked my husband for another pill, and as I sat in my chair, with the pill in my hand, I heard a voice from above say, "I have already healed you, so why are you taking that?" I knew right away what God was telling me. Within one day, I went from being addicted to some of the strongest narcotics to being addicted to absolutely nothing at all. Not once did I ever have any withdrawals, side effects, or anything. Our God has the power to deliver us from anything that we want to be delivered from. We just have to ask and receive it when He gives it to us.

God Is Not Just in Church

I owe a very special thank-you to Pastor Virgil Gene Limb, who married my husband and me on August 18, 2005. My husband and I stood on a balcony that overlooked Fort Gibson Lake, looking into each other's eyes as the pastor read us our vows. Gene also worked at our family funeral home. I will never forget the day he came into our funeral home and, with tears in his eyes, said, "I have been diagnosed with cancer." The next words from his mouth were "And my God will take care of me." Gene never once got sick while on chemotherapy, and he never had pain during his entire journey of sickness. Gene lived many months beyond the time in which the doctors gave him, and he knew that only God knows when it's time to go home. I always said if anyone deserved a golden pathway to heaven, it was Gene Limb. There was something so very special about him. His love for God radiated throughout his life here on earth. He kept every sermon that he preached. Throughout the years, there were many weddings, funerals, and baptisms delivered by him.

It was sometime after Gene's death and my return from heaven that I felt a calling to go to Chicago to visit with his wife and daughter, Kristi. When I arrived and told them my story, I let them know that somehow Pastor Gene had something to do with all of this. And they both replied that they know. Gene's daughter said, "I can see my dad in your eyes." During my stay, I had the opportunity to read some of the sermons Gene delivered during his lifetime. There was one of his sermons that stood out to me. And, a little later, I'll share with you what he wrote that became so special to me.

One encounter I had after our vacation and my healing had happened. I was standing in front of Walgreen's, returning one of the kids' movies that we had rented. A car pulled up behind me, and a very nice well-dressed woman got out of the car, and she stood behind me waiting until I was finished returning the movie. When I turned around, she said to me, "Ma'am, do you know where Shipman Funeral Home is?" I had been working at our Muskogee Funeral Home planting flowers and working around the shrubs in the yard. I was dressed in sweats and slightly embarrassed about the way I looked. I said, "Really?" and she replied yes and then asked why. I told her that my husband's parents own the funeral home and we all work there together. I asked her to follow me and I would take her there.

Once we arrived at the funeral home, she asked me if I would mind giving her the opportunity to take a tour of the funeral home. Without hesitation, I agreed, and we went inside. While midway through the tour of the funeral home, I still didn't know why she was so adamant about seeing our facilities, so I said to her, "May I ask why you're here?"

She replied, "Yes. I was at a Joyce Meyer Conference in Missouri. My husband was killed in an automobile accident on the Turner turnpike. I prayed to God this morning to please guide me to the right person to help me through this terrible time because I have never done this before and didn't know what to do."

Now that was an eye-opener. I thanked the woman so much for letting me know that she said that prayer that morning, and I thanked God for sending her to me for some comfort. I would have never known God had a reason for her and me to meet that night, but both of us left that meeting blessed by the touch of God.

The following is a sermon from Pastor Gene Limb, who had passed away in May of 2012. He is the one who asked God to give me a second chance when I was in heaven. This is only one scripture of many Gene wrote and tucked safely away in one of his shoeboxes. This is the one that made sense to me. It describes what I have experienced and how God has completely changed me from the person I used to be. You may ask why I so strongly believe that Gene had such a big part in God's plan with me. It's because Gene knew it would crush my husband to lose me. You see, my husband never left my side. He was always there to support and comfort me during my six-year battle of this illness. He pushed me to keep the faith when I felt that I couldn't go any further. I would tell him at night as we lay in bed, "I think I'm going to die soon, and I'm ready," but he would always respond, "No, you're not. It's going to be okay." Jason never lost hope. He always believed somehow I was going to get better and God wouldn't take me away from our family so soon. But I lost my hope.

Gene knew that I was tired. I was tired of the pain, the burden on my husband, and the financial strain on the family because of the doctor visits, medicine, and expensive tests. Gene knew I was ready to go, and I recall having a conversation with him about how I would go instead of him. While sick, Pastor Gene never had pain, but I hurt like crazy. My soul and body were tired. I'll never forget the day I returned home from a business trip to find that two young girls died that day in two separate automobile accidents. One girl was a soon-to-be high school graduate, and the other was a woman of my age, with two young children like mine. I was heartbroken and couldn't understand why God would not save them and just take me. I was ready; my kids understood that I was sick and not living a productive life. I was a broken child, a sinner, and I needed to be saved. Gene's body was tired, but his spirit was not. He always had a smile and a kind word. He was certain my salvation was near but my life would have many more years ahead of him because he too was certain God had special plans for my life. I'm certain that he convinced God to save me. I was blessed by him and saved by grace.

The night I called Gene's daughter and told her what happened to me, she said, "If my dad were here right now and you were telling him your story, he would have tears running down his face." Please enjoy the scripture below from the man who gave so much but asked for so little. With the permission of his wife and daughter, I will now share with you the writing of a very special man:

> Ye Must Be Born Again–John 3:1–7
>
> The 3rd verse of John 3 tells us, "Most assuredly, I say to you, unless one is born again, he cannot see the Kingdom of God."
>
> Have you been born again?
>
> Without it you have no hope of escaping the terrors of hell or enjoying the glories of heaven.
>
> I. What the New Birth is not
> 1. It is not a religion. Because Nicodemus was a Pharisee, a very strict religionist. He celebrated

the Passover, paid tithes, said his prayer, brought sacrifices, tried to keep the law to the letter. Yet it was to him Jesus said "ye must be born again."

2. It is not morality. You may go by the golden rule, pay your bills, be a good neighbor, stay out of jail, live a good moral life, but that will not save you.

3. It is not just changing your life and going to church every Sunday. That is not the New Birth!!! Your trouble is not on the outside but on the inside. It is not what people see on the outside but what God changes on the inside.

II. What the New Birth is

1. It is a mystery you cannot explain, but a reality no man can explain away. Just as Nicodemus could not understand or explain the wind, so no man can explain the New Birth…you would be a fool to say "I don't believe in the wind." I've never seen it, and therefore I cannot believe it.

2. It is the work of God by which a poor lost, guilty, hell deserving sinner who receives the Lord Jesus Christ receives a new nature. Becomes a child of God, and begins a new life.

3. It is the second birth; A spiritual birth. II Corinthians 5:17 "Therefore if any man be in Christ, he is a new creature: old things are passed away; behold, all things are become new."

III. Why must you be born again?

1. Because the Lord Jesus Christ said so.

2. Because you cannot save yourself. Ephesians 2:8-9 "For by grace are ye saved through faith; and that not of yourselves, it is the gift of God not of works, lest any man should boast.

IV. How to be born again (John 1:11–13)

1. It is not of blood line. You are not a Christian just because your parents are. You cannot inherit salvation from your parents.

2. It is not the will of the flesh. It is not by your own effort, you cannot save yourself.

3. It is of God, when an individual receives Christ, he is saved (John 1:12). But as many as received Him, to them He gave power to become the sons of God, even to them that believe on His name: Which were born, not of blood, nor of the will of the flesh, nor of the will of man, but of God. Galatians 3:26 "For ye are all the children of God by faith in Christ Jesus." Heaven or Hell—both are eternal life.

—(Written by Virgil Eugene Limb,
may your legacy here on earth forever live on.)

I know now that after spending months trying to remember exactly what happened and how it happened while we were on our trip, you will hear me use the words "I believe" many times because that is the only way I know how to explain what happened with truth.

I believe that when I said the words "I'm sorry, and I love you," I started the first transition out of my earthly body.

While my body was resting here on earth from 3:30 p.m. until 10:00 a.m. the next day, my soul and spirit were traveling through a place that not even I can translate into words. It was the most beautiful place that I have ever seen.

As I made my transitions, with the guidance of my angel, my soul and spirit traveled to the realm of God's kingdom. I will never forget how I felt while I was in the presence of my angel. He had the sweetest tone of voice, and you could feel the love and peace radiating from him. It was as though the way he moved and the noise he made, you knew exactly what he was saying without words. As soon as he spoke the words "It's going to be okay," I knew I could finally rest. While I was in heaven, I was shown things that no language here on earth can explain. It's by far the most glorious and peaceful place I had ever been.

While I was in heaven, there was a debate. I didn't quite understand what the debate was about, but it was a debate like I had never experienced before. It was a debate with the feeling of love and acceptance there. Just thinking of it brings a smile to my face. It's not like any debate any of us have experienced here on earth. There were a lot of people around me while the debate was going on. There were people I knew and people I had never seen before. It felt like it lasted for what seemed like hours compared to our earthly time. But when the debate was over, I realized what was going to happen when the Lord looked at me with His eyes that are filled with a love I had never known or seen until that time. He looked at me and said, "You have to go back." I begged

Him not to let me go. I didn't want to leave. For the first time, I was at peace and absolutely loved where I was, but the Lord told me I had to go back and tell the people that God is real and that He is a loving and a forgiving God. Then He said, "But you won't be there long, because I'm going to come back and get you, along with everyone else." Even after the Lord sent me back, it really didn't sink in or wasn't revealed to me exactly what He was wanting me to do until a couple of months later.

It wasn't until January of 2013 when I received the baptism of the Holy Ghost. The Lord told me it was time to tell the story of my journey. The six years of pain, dying, my time in heaven, and the message He sent me back to proclaim to America. He is coming soon. Then one day God gave me a wonderful tool to help me share this story. Something so amazing only God could have put it in my path.

So in January, I began writing about what I had gone through for six years, my time in heaven, and the message I had received. It didn't seem to take me long to write the first part of the book since I had actually lived it, and I already knew how that part of the story went, so that part of the book was completed in March of that year. I didn't know how God was going to work everything out with the book and the message He had given to me until June of 2013. That's when He delivered the beginning key part to this book to help prove to America that Christ is indeed coming back to get us.

The Rock: God's Message
to America

Before I was sent back from heaven, I begged the Lord to please not send me back. He told me I had to go back and tell people that God is real, loving, and forgiving, but I won't be there long because He was going to come back and get me, along with everyone else. I knew with the society that we live in today not everyone would believe my story, much less the message that the Lord had given to me. So I prayed on it for many nights, and finally, during one of my prayers, He spoke to me and said, "When this is all said and done, you only have one judge, and that's me."

After that, I have always had great peace, because it's the absolute truth. No one on this earth has the right to judge me or anyone else, except for God. But I still wondered how

I was going to deliver the message and be able to prove to others that we do indeed have a loving and forgiving God. But God knew the entire time how He was going to put everything together and show people what the message that He had given me to deliver to America meant.

In June of 2013, my family and I had decided to go back to Roaring River in Cassville, Missouri, to take pictures for the book, since this is where I experienced heaven and my new life began. While we were there, my son and I decided to go for a walk down the riverbank. On this particular weekend, there were a lot of people since the park was hosting free fishing for children that weekend. As we were walking down the riverbank, I stubbed my toe on a rock. I let out a yell. My son picked up the rock and said, "Wow, Mom. Look, this is awesome."

As I looked at it, I could tell it had to be a gift from God but was not quite sure what kind of gift. At first glance, the rock was extremely unique, on the bottom it has a hole in it with perfectly cut stones shaped like diamonds. The hole resembles Jesus's tomb, where He was laid after He was crucified on the cross. On the top of the rock is a symbol showing a side profile of a man's face in the sun rays, which represents Christ coming down from the clouds (1 Thessalonians 4:16, NIV). At that particular time, I had no clue what the rock meant or that it had so many different seals on it that unfolded the story of Revelation. It has taken several months to unlock the story of the rock with the help of the Holy Ghost and the Lord.

As I mentioned earlier, I had gone back to the place to take pictures for the book. At that time, I just assumed God wanted me to write a book about my illness, my time in heaven, the healing I received, and the message. But I was wrong. I have learned during my walk with God that oftentimes we step on stones that were not intended for us to step on, and we receive lessons from our heavenly Father so He can guide us in the right direction and get us back on course. It was one month prior to what I thought was the completed book to be published when I received my whipping and a lesson. I had chosen a publishing company that God did not intend for me to use during this time, and problems started arising that shouldn't have. I knew right away I had made a wrong decision, so I began to pray and seek God for answers to what I had done wrong and what He wanted me to do. He told me, "The rock, it has a story."

My heart dropped. I had no clue what type of story this rock could possibly have, but over the course of four months, the Lord and Holy Ghost have revealed it to me, along with my dear friend Sharron, who has spent countless hours working with me. The story the rock reveals is absolutely amazing and glorious, but it can also be scary if you don't know Jesus Christ as your Lord and Savior. This rock speaks the truth about the powerful gospel of Jesus Christ. I was told I wouldn't be here long because Jesus would come back and get me, along with everyone else. And the rock shows exactly what I was told and how the Gospel began and how it's going to end.

I was in a Christian bookstore one day, and I met a gentleman whom I believe was one of God's angels. He prophesized over me, and I showed him the rock, and he said, "That rock is a rock of prophesy." God is trying to get America's attention. This book is not about me but about God and what He's done for me and what He is telling America so their hearts and souls will be right before His Son, Jesus Christ, comes to get us.

I didn't receive the final part of the rock, which completed the story until October of 2013, which shows how the Gospel began. Everything started with God: our universe, our creation, absolutely everything. "In the beginning God created the heavens and the earth" (Genesis 1:1, NIV). God is our light. He's a spiritual being of love, but people don't believe in Him because they can't physically touch Him.

I had gone back to Roaring River in October of 2013 with just my husband to get away and write on the book. One Saturday evening, I was in the cabin, and the Lord told me to go for a walk and take a flashlight. So my husband and I started off on our walk, not sure where the Lord was leading us to, but we ended up back at the same part of the river where we had found the first rock. I bent down, and there was a white rock with a cross right in the middle, and on the side of it is a face. The most amazing part of the white rock is when you shine a light under the bottom of it, it glows and radiates a light like nothing else here on earth.

The white rock shows how the Gospel began. The light and glow that shines through the rock represents God and how He is our light and a spiritual being. The cross and the face on the rock represent Jesus Christ and how God sent His one and only begotten Son to teach us the gospel so that we would walk in love and peace and seek God for help and the answers we need. People mocked God's Son as He went out upon the earth speaking the gospel and showing the miracles that He could perform because He had the Spirit of God in Him. After walking the earth for three and a half years, He was hung on a cross and crucified. Just before Jesus died, He said, "It is finished," which meant, and still means, that everything He had done we would be able to do through Him and the scriptures. Then He was carried to the tomb, where He laid for three days before His Father God resurrected Him from the dead and took Him into heaven.

The white rock is perfectly cut and shaped so that it sits right over the tomb on the back of the big rock. It shows and tells the story of how the stone was rolled away and the tomb was empty (Luke 24:1-8, NIV). But this tomb is not empty. It is filled with perfectly cut stones, and no matter where the rock is, the stones in the tomb always radiate light. That is because Jesus is also our light. In the back of the book you will find illustrations of the rock that was delivered to me as a tool to proclaim the message.

While Jesus was here on earth, He told us to walk in love and peace, to cast down our nets and follow Him. To the right of the tomb is a dove. The dove represents love, peace and the Holy Spirit. In the middle of the dove is a fish, which represents "Cast down your nets and follow me." The dove and fish tell us what Jesus told us to do not only in the beginning but also now, which is to cast down the things of the world and follow Him so we can have love, peace, and everlasting life. Everything that Jesus taught His disciples and the people was the truth, and everything that was written in the Bible will be fulfilled. "I am the way and the truth and the life. No one comes to the Father except through me" (John 14:6, NIV).

On the top of the rock, it shows what's to happen and take place before Christ's return. On the top right, there is a set of dove wings, which symbolize the Holy Spirit and how God said "I will pour out my spirit on all people" (Acts 2:17, NIV). To the left of the dove wings is a pig's face. The pig goes back to the parable of the lost son in Luke 15:11–32. It is written that in the final days that people will turn from God for wealth and the things of the world. And that is exactly what has happened, but God is saying to His children, "Turn back to me. Repent and accept my Son, Jesus Christ, into your heart, and I will give you a place in heaven." To the left of the pig's face is a faint face on the top left of the rock. In the last days, scoffers will come, scoffing and following their own evil desires. They will say, "Where is this coming He promised?" (2 Peter 3:3–4, NIV). There will also be false teachers among us.

Right in the middle of the upper part of the rock, above the cloud, is satan. In the final days, evil will be all over the world, and that is exactly what we have now. People turning on people, killing each other and God's innocent babies. But satan is another truth to the Gospel of Jesus Christ. In the very beginning, he deceived Adam and Eve while they were in the garden (Genesis 3:1–14, NIV). That's exactly what he is doing today, and has been doing for years. He is destroying the souls of God's children right before Christ's return. As children of God, we need to be bold and stand up and start saving the souls of the ones who are lost. Jesus is coming (1 Thessalonians 4:16, NIV). "For the Lord himself will come down from heaven, with a loud command, with the voice of the archangel, and with the trumpet call of God, and the dead in Christ will rise first."

On the rock, right below satan, is a cloud with Christ's face right in the middle of the rays, and under Christ is a person's body. I believe if Christ were to come today there would be a lot of souls going through tribulation. But God loves us all; in God's eyes, we are all equal. It doesn't matter what title you have for a career, if you're a physician, preacher, trash truck driver, clerk, or a homeless person. God sees us all the same and knows where our hearts are. Satan has deceived many people into not teaching or writing the truth about the Gospel of Jesus Christ. There is only one gospel and one truth, and that's the Word of God. It doesn't matter what ethnicity or religion you are. What's in your heart is what matters to God, and we must know and accept that Jesus Christ is our Lord and Savior. We have to believe in God's Son to have our place in heaven.

On the bottom of the rock, right below the symbol of the return of Christ, starting on the left shows a woman's face looking down with a sad expression, and right above her is an opossum. Everything on the rock is found in the Bible or has a prophetic meaning, but the opossum is the one that really stumped me. I searched the Bible and prophetic books and found absolutely nothing about an opossum, but it does indeed fit into the story of Revelation. It is stated that in the end times, the church will be asleep. We, the people, are the church, and what does an opossum do? It plays like it's dead or asleep. It's sad because people are not waking up to the warnings that God has already given to us.

To the right of the crack on the bottom half of the rock is a goat and a ram. The goat symbolizes destruction, and the ram symbolizes war. In the final days, we will experience destruction and war on our earth. On the left side of the rock is a lamb, and to the right of the lamb is a cow. The forehead of the cow has clear stones in it. The stones and cow represent Israel, because she has always been God's most chosen nation, and America was second. Israel used to sacrifice the lamb and the red heifers, so what has America done that Israel did? We have turned our backs on God, have mocked Him, and have taken Him out of our lives, so what part of our body will be judged? Our hearts. To the right of the cow is a heart, and right below the heart is a face, with tears coming out of the eyes. This is going to be a sad day for the ones who don't wake up to God's warnings.

As I have mentioned before, not once have I ever read the Bible until after my experience of going to heaven. But once the Holy Spirit started revealing to me the symbols on the rock, I started really digging into the Word of God to figure out what story He was telling me. One thing I have discovered is that in America and across the world, we have several different versions of the Bible and every scripture is worded differently. I praise God every day for the gift of the Holy Spirit. This book and my testimony would have never been possible if it wasn't for the Holy Ghost guiding me.

I believe once we see evil rise in our world like we have never seen before and witness crimes committed we never thought could possibly happen is when we will see Christ appear.

> At that time they will see the Son of Man coming in a cloud with power and great glory. When these things begin to take place, stand up and lift up your heads, because your redemption is drawing near.
>
> Luke 21:27–28, NIV

Oh, what a glorious day that will be; just writing it gets my spirit excited. To a lot of people, this day scares them, and I believe it's because they have never been taught the truth and don't understand that this is not where our lives end. We all must understand that God loves each and every one of us and desires nothing more than to welcome us home in heaven. Now is the time to get our hearts right with God, and if your heart is right, now is the time to stand up for God and His Son, Jesus Christ, and preach the powerful Gospel of Jesus Christ on the streets, stores, or wherever you are. Be the person who plants that seed to bring home one of God's lost children. If you are a child of God, you have nothing to worry about because we are covered in the Blood of Jesus, and we will be protected until the day He returns. Jesus stood up for us and died on the cross for each and every one of us. So now is the time we stand up and stop letting satan put fear in our lives. God loves us all so much and wants to forgive us that He is showing us through this rock what is going to take place in America.

Tribulation

After the dead in Christ and all the believers are gone, the ones who were asleep or played opossum to the warnings and messages God had sent will go through tribulation. Tribulation will last for seven years. There will be an antichrist that is going to come in the form of Christ and promise peace, tell lies, and show great miracles. Although he is going to bring peace for the first three and a half years, it's still going to be a sad day for the ones who didn't listen to what they were told and for the ones who didn't teach the true gospel and misled God's children. In our nation already we have many false prophets and people who do not speak the truth. Satan is an ugly creature and will deceive whoever he can to keep them from going to heaven and enjoying a glorious everlasting life. The ones who are left behind are going to have to seek God and stay strong in their faith so they are not deceived, just like the believers are doing today. After the three and a half years of peace, the Armageddon war will begin. The four horses of tribulation will be released; the war, destruction, and famine will start and will last for the remaining three and a half years.

If you look at the picture of the rock, under the symbol of Christ's return, you will see the white horse (Revelation 6:2, NIV). "I looked, and there before me was a white horse!" Its rider held a bow, and he was given a crown, and he rode out as a conqueror bent on conquest. Behind the white horse is the fiery red horse. "When the Lamb opened the second seal, I heard the second living creature say, 'Come!' Then another horse came out, a fiery red one. Its rider was given power to take peace from the earth and to make men slay each other" (Revelation 6:3–4, NIV). Then comes the black horse. "When the Lamb opened the third seal, I heard the third living creature say, 'Come!' I looked, and there before me was a black horse! Its rider was holding a pair of scales in his hand. Then I heard what sounded like a voice among the four living creatures, saying, 'A quart of wheat for a day's wages, and three quarts of barley for a day's wages and do not damage the oil and wine!'" (Revelation 6:5–6, NIV). If you look behind the red horse, you will see a face with its mouth open like it is hungry. Finally comes the pale horse. "When the Lamb opened the fourth seal, I heard the voice of the fourth living creature say, 'Come!' I looked, and there before me was a pale horse! Its rider was named Death, and Hades was following close behind him. They were given power over a fourth of the earth to kill by sword, famine, plague, and by the wild beasts of the earth" (Revelation 6:7–8). If you look to the left of the pale horse, you will see the face of a young adult boy, who appears that his arms have been cut off. In this time people, will be killed because of the Word of God and the testimony they had maintained (Revelation 6:9, NIV).

During this time, the mark of the beast will come into the scene and try to deceive people into taking the mark so they can buy, sell, or trade food to survive with. If they are deceived, he will put a mark on either their heads or hands. If you receive the mark, you will be able to eat, trade, or sell food for the time that's left during tribulation. It will make it easier to survive, but you won't get to heaven. During this time you are going to have to be strong in your faith and stand up for God. The people who are not deceived and stand up will lose their lives, but the reward is everlasting life in heaven with God, Jesus Christ, and the Holy Ghost. The torture people are going to face during the time of tribulation is tremendous, and they will hide in caves. They called to the mountains and the rocks, "Fall on us and hide us from the face of him who sits on the throne and from the wrath of the Lamb" (Revelation 6:16, NIV).

Under the rock I found someone hiding in a cave, and faces that look like they were burnt. I can't imagine why anyone would want to ignore the warnings and God's message to go through seven years of pain. I can't imagine the heartache that parents will feel when they realize that their children are nowhere to be found because the children who are not of age to be accountable for their sins will be automatically taken to heaven during the rapture. Or the old who, because they have heard of Christ's coming since they were children, didn't wake up to the signs, and turn their lives over to the Lord will also be left behind. God is giving each and every one of us a choice to go as soon as the trumpet calls. If you can't live for God and accept Jesus Christ as your Savior today with the love and mercy we have upon the earth now, how do you expect to live when it will be life or death? What is on earth is nothing compared to what is waiting for us in heaven. The people in our nation have become absorbed with the things of the world, especially money. But you have to realize at this time God is giving us a choice: we can either turn back and repent and accept Jesus into our hearts or continue into the things of the world and be left behind and witness things we never thought could happen. God is tired of being rejected and of people mocking Him and His Son. He has given us life, yet people would much rather believe in something that's not true or worship idols.

After discovering the seals on the rock and what God is trying to tell His children in America, I have worked countless hours to pull the story together. God is showing America we have done exactly what Israel did: we turned from Him. He has warned us and asked us to turn back and repent, but we never did. Now our day of judgment is coming. It's going to be a sad day for those who didn't listen.

During these past four months, I have spent much time seeking God and listening to what the Holy Ghost was telling me. I had no clue as to how God wanted me to write the story on the rock, if I was to put scriptures, with all the seals. But the more I sought God and read the Word, the more I discovered that the truth of what's going to happen has already been written with the scriptures and very few people seek God anymore, so instead of Him giving the story again with scriptures, He is showing His children what's going to happen with the seals on the rock. God is revealing the signs of Christ's return and what is going to take place so people will begin to seek Him. Revelation is very difficult to understand and extremely hard to write about. Never in a million years did I think I would be writing this book. But we never know who God is going to use to speak to us or how He's going to show us the answers to our prayers. He has used people whom I have known for many years to tell me what I needed to hear or to show me some of the seals on the rock.

After receiving the rock, I prayed several times for the Lord to show me what the seal on the top of the rock meant, and finally, one night He showed me in a dream. In my dream, I was at the office, and there were three men in front of me. One man was in a wheelchair, and he had one guy on each side of him. I had shared with them my testimony and showed them the rock, and the guy standing on the right looked at me and pointed to the seal on the top of the rock and said, "Do you know what that means?" I said no then he pointed to a window that was behind me and said, "Look." When I turned around and looked, it was Christ coming down out of the clouds, and he told me, "Always remember one thing: you can't be pushy. You have to be gentle." Two days later, I was actually working visitation at the office when a gentleman came in. I was talking about the rock to one of the family members who had lost their loved one when the man who told me what the symbol on the rock meant in my dream appeared. I was standing with my back to him and I was holding the rock in my hand when he came up behind me and said, "Wow, look at all of those seals. They all have meaning." I was absolutely amazed and felt extremely blessed that God would send someone to me to help me understand what He wanted me to know.

One thing I have learned during this time is that the people in this world today are searching for love, happiness, joy, and peace, but they can't find it because they are turning to the world and not to God. God is where you receive your love, joy, and happiness. This world can't give you any of those things. It's time we cast down the world and find our salvation and follow Jesus Christ. It's time to stop chasing the world and letting satan destroy our children, marriages, and lives. It's time to accept Jesus Christ into our hearts so we don't have to go through the dark times of tribulation.

A month after receiving the rock from God, I took a picture of it to send to a friend who lives out of state. So for three months, several of my other close friends and I looked at the pictures, and I had even handed them out at churches where I have shared my testimony. But it wasn't until October of 2013—the day before our government came to a temporary agreement about health care—that the Lord revealed to my friend Sharron and me the images on the picture that show exactly what's going to happen during the time of tribulation. I believe God waited to reveal the images of tribulation because He was giving us a chance to turn back and repent during the time that the government was shut down. We don't need the government to give us our health care; our health is through God and the power of prayer. But instead of turning to God, our nation continued to turn to man. God is showing us the truth of what people who are living in the darkness and not waking up to the signs will experience.

There are two truths to the Gospel of Jesus Christ. The first is about God and His Son, and the second is about satan. People don't believe God is real; therefore, they don't believe satan is real. But satan is the ugly truth; he's a snake and goes around deceiving people and destroying their souls. Ever since I was a child I heard people talk about ghosts or spirits, I always had a fear of them even though I never knew if they were real or make-believe. During the time of me writing the book, I have prayed and asked God to show me the truths of the Gospel because everyone has their own beliefs. God has shown me many of the amazing and glorious truths, like being baptized in the Holy Ghost, speaking in tongues, being slain in the Spirit, and many more, but He has also shown me the truth of the ugly side, which is satan. I now know that God sends His Holy Spirit to us to guide each and every one of us on our journey. Many times we are entertaining angels and don't even know it until they are gone. I also know that satan will cast out his evil spirits among people, especially the ones who are working for God, to try to deceive them and make them backslide.

Satan knew what really sent fear to my heart because, like I said, ever since I was a child, I have always had a fear of ghosts, and working in the funeral business, I would pray that I would never see one. But while working on this book, I have discovered that satan will cast out his spirits on the people closest to you in hopes to bring you down, where you won't complete your job for God. My husband and I have been together for fifteen years now, and we have always had a good relationship. We've had our ups and downs, but for the most part, we never had any problems agreeing on things. But once I started working for God and following Jesus, we had more disagreements than ever before. Jason and I had the discussion many of times how it was weird that while I was sick and of all the things we had gone through, we never seemed to have as many disagreements as we did now. So what changed? We have God in us and we listen to what He is telling us to do, and satan doesn't like it.

Jason and I were at church on a Wednesday, and I began to notice that every time we would go to church or I was scheduled to speak somewhere, something was always coming against me. While sitting in church this particular Wednesday, I noticed my husband wasn't acting like himself. He seemed very unhappy, and I could feel the negativity radiating from him. As the praise and worship was going on, the Holy Ghost spoke to me and said, "Go outside." Not knowing what for, I went, and I began to pray and ask God to please just touch my husband and bring him peace about the new life that God had laid out for us. The Lord spoke to my heart and said, "It's a bad spirit."

I wasn't sure what that meant until I got home from church. The kids and Jason were in bed, and I was sitting on my couch, pondering on the idea of writing and figuring out how I was going to be able to work for God and still have the man whom I fell in love with fifteen years ago be by my side. All of a sudden, this woman's face, with real dark evil eyes, appeared. She said, "You are going on this walk alone." Chills ran all over my body. All I could do was start pleading the blood of Jesus over me and my family. I knew right then that was what the Lord was telling me that night during church. I now know that satan will cast out his spirits to try to destroy your marriage when you are doing what God wants you to do. People need to be educated about how satan works and the tactics he uses to destroy God's children.

The closer I got to finishing the book and the more that was revealed to me on the rock, the more the enemy tried to attack me with his spirits. He tries everything he can to stop the saints from completing the task that God has laid out for them to do. Satan's going to continue to cast out his evil spirits among our nation until the day that Christ returns. Praise God we are covered in the Blood of Jesus and the evil spirits can't touch us, but we have got to continue to seek God in prayer and stay strong until the final day comes. Satan is a snake, and he will try his hardest to squirm his way into your home to destroy your relationship with your children, spouse, and anyone you love; he won't bother you as long as you're doing what he wants you to do, but if you're working for God, watch out.

Satan is destroying the churches today with his evil spirits, and we are allowing it to happen. We need more fasting and praying going on now more than ever so we can overcome what he is trying to put on us. Evil spirits are just as real and exist, just like God and Jesus Christ. If you turn the picture of the rock upside down and look on the left side, you will see a snake that looks like it's alive, because satan is alive and real; he's the ugly truth. The ones who are deceived by satan will go through the darkness of tribulation. God loves us all so much that He is showing us what's going to come and what's going to happen to us if we don't accept the salvation that belongs to us. He knows that there are people who are not preaching the truth and who don't listen to what the Holy Spirit is telling them to do. God has delivered this rock to me to warn America of the coming of Jesus. The message I received is not mine but everyone's; I was just chosen to deliver the message for God. If you rotate the picture to the right and look on the upper left-hand corner, you will see an old man with white hair, and to his left is a demonic creature with pointy ears. But if you turn the picture back upright, in the same corner you will see a wolf with half of a man's face to the right. This rock, indeed, has a story to tell. It tells how it all began and how it's going to end. It also shows the truths in the Gospel.

The Bible is very complicated, and how one person perceives a scripture it means something totally different to the next. Some people are filled with the Holy Ghost, whereas others are not, so everyone sees things differently. I will be completely honest: if I had never received this rock, I would not know what I know now about Revelation. For one, it's extremely hard to understand, and second, it's scary to hear about what's going to happen. I never knew it was true that one day Christ would come and we would face judgment, and if we were left behind, people would be killed and go through such calamity. I had no idea that could even happen. I had heard about it once or twice but thought that the ones who said it were crazy, until I went to heaven and was given the message to tell people we have a forgiving and loving God and that He would come back and get me, along with everyone else. Even then, I still didn't know to what extent Revelation went to until I received the rock and spent hours in the Word and Spirit searching and seeking God for the answers.

After searching the Bible for the scriptures to put with the rock, I have discovered that everything on this rock is in the Bible and reveals Revelation. But after months of searching in the Word and seeking God, I became confused and frustrated. I knew the Lord told me the rock had a story and He showed it to me, but I couldn't figure out how He wanted me to write it. The more I searched in the Word, the deeper and more complicated it became for me to write. And finally, after hitting my breaking point, the Lord revealed to me through the Holy Ghost that I'm not to explain every seal on this rock with Scriptures. The Scriptures have already been given to us, and it would only confuse people, especially the ones who know nothing about God or Jesus Christ. Every seal on the rock is in the Bible and has a scripture that goes with it, and you might ask, how do you know that they are seals? I know this because God sent one of his angels to me at the very beginning of me trying to discover what the rock meant to let me know so I would search and seek out the rest of the meaning of the rock. God has revealed the seals on this rock through the Holy Ghost, by sending angels to me, and even through my dreams.

I spend a lot of time in prayer seeking God for answers I know only He can give me. I had been praying and asking God to reveal to me the name of the rock and what part of the Bible did the story come from, and one night, in a dream, He showed me Revelation. I've had Jesus come to my bedside right before I was to speak at a church. I had been praying, asking the Lord what it was He wanted me to share with the church that Sunday, my testimony or the rock. Two nights before I was to speak, at one thirty in the morning, Jesus appeared at my bedside and said, "I have placed in your heart what I want you to say on Sunday." I woke up when I heard Him speak, and I saw Him walking away from my bed. I have learned that if we are obedient to God and if we listen to what He is telling us, He will give us the answers and the desires of our hearts that we are searching for.

It's not easy to walk with God and be obedient. But by God's grace and mercy, I have made it this far, and I'm not turning back. If I can do it, anyone can do it. The blessings that God sends your way are amazing when you listen to Him.

He has taught me how to separate myself from the world and to be thankful for the little things in life.

In order for me to be able to show what every seal means, you would need to actually see the rock because of how God has placed them on it. And with the picture, you have to turn it in so many different directions that it would be impossible for me to explain in writing how to turn it and find what I am talking about. So my job for this book is to tell you about the message I received, show you the key symbols on the rock, and tell you what story lies behind them. Who is the rock? Jesus Christ, our salvation, the foundation of our lives. If we deny the rock (Jesus), we deny God, and no man who doesn't believe in His Son, Jesus, can go to God. By receiving this rock, it has given me the desire to seek God more and to find the truth in what everything means. And that's what God wants America to do: to seek His face to turn from the world and repent so all His children will come home. God loves us all the same, and He created each and every one of us for a purpose.

We all have a testimony on how God has touched our lives and delivered us from a place where we needed help. Now is the time to start sharing our testimonies and telling people just exactly how God has touched you and raised you up when no one else was there for you. We all must understand we are who we are and have what we have because of God and the sacrifice that Jesus Christ made for us. No one here on earth is going to get you to heaven; it's up to you to do the work. God is saying, "It's time to make a decision. Let me know if you want to accept my Son, Jesus Christ, the Rock, or deny Him." We can't see God because He is a spiritual being; therefore, people refuse to believe in Him. But God has given us a rock to believe in with all the signs of Christ's return and what's going to take place after the rapture.

I don't know when Christ will return, and no one else will either. Only God knows when He's going to send His Son back to get us. I do know that God keeps every promise He makes, and I don't think we have much longer, and God is telling us to wake up and stop playing possum to the signs He is showing us. Our world needs repentance, love, peace, and fear of the Lord. We need people praying and seeking the face of God and to know this is not where it ends.

We are promised everlasting life, and we have a choice: do we want a glorious everlasting life in the kingdom of God or an everlasting life of torture in the lake of fire with satan? Heaven is the most peaceful and glorious place we will ever know. There's nothing this world could offer to keep me from going back to heaven. I have more joy, happiness, peace, and love now than I have ever had, and I don't get it from the world but from God, because He lives in me.

The day that I was baptized in the Holy Spirit, I said, "I'm going to write a book, and everyone who reads it will be successful." People today view success as money, but what God means is you will have a place in heaven. I thought the first part of this book was hard, but I was wrong. I believe the second part was even harder because I had to learn the story where I actually lived the first part of this book. God has absolutely amazed me on how He has pulled everything together including the people He has placed in my life to help with it. I could have never completed this book without them.

I praise and thank God every day for saving me with His grace and mercy, for showing me His love, and for guiding me through this entire process. I never dreamed I would have a second chance in life, much less feel healthy again or have a story like the one God has trusted with me. I am so thankful, and for that, I will always put God first in my life. I will stand up for what I know is the truth, even if I have to stand alone. I will never turn my back on God, Jesus, or the Holy Ghost. I will shout the powerful Gospel of Jesus Christ until the day I return back home to my heavenly Father. Because the truth is I wouldn't be here today if it wasn't for God; none of us would. I've had to tell the ones whom I love that I'm going to follow Jesus and walk away from places in my life where I thought I would always be.

But through it all, God has carried me through it and was there to catch me when I was falling. He has disciplined me and molded me into the person He wants me to be so I can finish the final journey He has set out for me to complete for Him. I was speaking at a church in Tahlequah, Oklahoma, one Sunday evening, and after sharing my testimony and showing the rock, a woman came up to me with tears in her eyes.

"I can't explain it," she said. "But when you were holding the rock up, showing us the tomb, I saw a lion."

She asked if I had ever shone a light into the hole to see what would show on the other side, and I said no. So when I got home, I grabbed a flashlight and shined it into the hole, and what appeared on the other side was absolutely astonishing. It showed a playful lion wearing a crown, with his paw stretched out. It is said that when all is said in done, the lion and the lamb will lie down with the children and play. That God will bring down the new heaven in Jerusalem and the believers will worship God, Jesus, and the Holy Ghost. In the face of the lion are three other faces, which represent the Father, Son, and Holy Ghost. Below the lion is what looks like fire, with a face trapped in it on the bottom left, and to the right of the face is an image that looks like a serpent. This is representing hell. This image is the one on the front cover of the book.

God is showing us the truth, that heaven and hell are indeed real. God has shown and revealed to me some amazing things in the past year and a half, and one thing that I have learned is there is only one person who knows the absolute truth to everything and the timing to when events are going to occur in our nation, and that's God. God has delivered this rock to open the eyes of His children who are asleep. He is showing us what is going to take place and what will happen after Christ comes. God has placed and is showing us very distinct faces that have specific characteristics. He loves us so much that He is showing the ones who are left behind after the rapture who to watch out for so they are not deceived.

There is going to be an antichrist, false prophets, and the mark of the beast, who is going to try and deceive the people of God who stand up for Him. Only one person at this time knows the truth of who these people are and where they fit into the time of tribulation, and that's God. But for the ones who don't listen to God's message and turn back and repent, they will find out the truth of who they are after the rapture. But God is saying, "I love you so much I am warning you now who will come to try and deceive you."

In order to receive what we pray for, we have to be true believers and believe that God is real and alive. Why should God grant us what we pray for if we don't believe in Him and do what He is asking us to do? God wants us to talk about Him and share with each other the amazing gifts He has given us and how He has worked in our lives.

God is loving and forgiving and will give us whatever our hearts desire, but first we have to accept His Son as our Lord and Savior and believe that whatever and whoever we pray for will be answered.

Everyone's walk with God is different; not everyone will experience what others do. That's because God has a plan for each of us, but we need to share our personal experiences with other people and not judge each other because of the way God works and performs in their lives. Since God has saved me and allowed me a second chance to make my life right, I have experienced some awesome acts of God. Things I couldn't explain or wasn't sure if I wanted to share with other people in fear of what they would think. But I know our job is to share what God does in our lives to help inspire others who may be losing their way.

I have come to realize in different churches that God has taken me. Many of God's children have been taught the opposite of what He intended for them to learn. We, as a nation, need to get back to teaching the true Gospel of Jesus Christ and not what our flesh believes is true. God has shown me the true Gospel versus what people believe the Bible means. It can be very confusing to know the truth from the false. We have turned our churches into businesses instead of a place to worship God. Churches have stopped letting the spirit of God move. Some only allow the speaking of tongues when they don't have any visitors. We can't just turn God off and on when we want to, people need to know the truth and how powerful it is to be baptized by the fire of the Holy Ghost. But for some reason, we have people who are scaring people out of the churches by what they are preaching. We have people who are worried about what others will think of them if they go to the altar or if they can't afford to pay tithes. No one should be judging anyone. If we see that someone is having a hard time, we should turn our hearts over to God and pray for them instead of judging them.

I have seen people go to church, and before they can even get out the doors, they are talking about what someone said or did. This is another reason why our church buildings are empty today, because people who claim to be Christians treat people horribly. God desires nothing more than for all His children to come together as one. How will we ever touch the lost souls if we can't even agree to the truth that was taught to us through Jesus Christ?

Do bad things happen in the churches today? Yes, but we must understand that God will take care of the person or persons who are doing wrong. Instead of trying to take care of the problem ourselves, we need to turn to God and pray and trust in Him and know that He will fix the problem. We have got to stop being defiant and help the souls that are outside and inside the church that are lost. This is our job as children of God. We are all equal, but for some reason, in today's society, we have come to the conclusion that if our church is bigger or if we have more money than someone else, we are more important. That's not true.

I work in a business where I am around a lot of preachers, church people, and people who do not attend church. I know now from my own personal experience and from seeing how other people talk and act about others why our churches are empty today. Our job is not to judge others but to love them and help them in their walk with God, but for some reason, we have allowed our flesh to get in the way, and we only want to believe in what we believe. It was never intended for us to have segregated churches or to be judging people on what gift God anointed another person with.

I have been to several churches trying to figure out where I belonged. People would ask what denomination I was, and I couldn't tell them because I didn't know what Baptist, Pentecostal, Methodist, or any other denomination meant. But the Lord showed me He's not about religion but about love and salvation, so I just simply tell people I'm a child of God. I have learned that a lot of people don't understand the true Gospel of Jesus Christ and how powerful it is. I have attended churches where, during the entire service, the people in the congregation never moved. We need to get up and shout God's name and praise Him for everything He has done in our lives. I know from my experience and how God has moved in my life and my family that we have an awesome big God and when I attend church, I want to get up and praise Him for all He'd done and is doing for me.

Because of what some people were taught, they try to keep God in a box and don't allow the Spirit to move through the church. God is too big to be put in a box! Just because you attend a church that has a particular label on the building doesn't mean you shouldn't worship and praise God. We, as humans, have put labels on our churches. God never mentioned Catholics, Baptists, Methodists, or any other religion in His book. We have named and labeled ourselves.

Have you ever attended church and felt more alive when you entered than when you left? If so, this is when you know you are in a church or are being taught the Word by someone who is not anointed to be a preacher.

After attending several different churches, I was amazed that my husband and I were almost always the youngest ones there. So I asked God one day why this was and why churches are so empty. Some churches don't even have a Sunday evening service, much less Wednesday night. God revealed to me one of the reasons was because years ago, we started having classes for our children to attend while we worshipped God. When we started sending our children to a different room, we were keeping our children from seeing what God does and how the Holy Spirit moves in the church. So when our children get of age to be moved to the sanctuary, they don't know how to accept the acts of God that are performed.

Our children learn from their parents and the people they are around. If they never witness us worshipping God and going to the altar for whatever reason, how will they know what to do when they become adults? For years, we thought we were doing the right thing by sending our children to classrooms, but what we were doing, and are still doing today, is sheltering our children from witnessing what God can do. The devil has over the years gradually wedged his way into God's buildings and destroyed people's faith.

As parents, we should make sure that wherever we attend church and if our children do go into a classroom, they are being educated on the importance of knowing God and the truths in His Word. It was a couple of months after my healing, I was at home alone with both of our children. My daughter went outside without shoes into the front yard. After a few minutes, she came in the house, crying, and she had blood dripping from her foot. I sat her down and examined her foot, and I could feel a sharp piece of glass in the middle of her foot where the blood was coming from, so I asked my son to run out to my car and get my tweezers.

While he was outside, something came over me. I still had her foot in my hand, so I began to pray over her foot, and when I did, the most amazing sensation started running through my body and tears started flowing out of my eyes. When I finished my prayer and opened my eyes, my daughter's foot was completely healed. The blood and glass were gone. I was shocked, amazed, and confused at what had just happened. I knew whatever had happened wasn't of me but of God. We are His vessels to reach out and touch those in need. Ever since that day and ever since Addison witnessed what God did to her foot, if anyone in our family gets hurt, she prays over them and asks God to heal them.

Our children learn and grow into who God wants them to be by learning from us. God is still in the healing business today, just as He was in the very beginning when it all started. Every night, when I lay my children in bed, either me or my husband will pray over them and ask God to protect them and allow them to have peaceful dreams. In the car going to school, we pray together for God to send His angels and watch over them while there at school and to keep the evil out of their lives and only allow in the people who will love them.

We encourage our children to pray at school in hopes that they will plant a seed of God into another child. It's very important to tell our children, friends, coworkers, and people we encounter during the day about God and the promises He made to us. We are living in the final days before the return of Christ, and when He returns, He's going to take the true believers home. You might get up and speak about God or preach out of the Bible, but are you a true believer, and are you teaching God's sheep the true Word or what you believe the truth is? While I was in heaven and after what felt like a debate was over, I realized that not only did God decide to save me but also I was chosen to come back for a specific reason.

God has been trying and is still trying to wake His children up to what is soon to happen, but we're not listening. We have got to stop worrying about the worldly things and start listening to what God is telling us if we want to go on the first trip. Start teaching the true Gospel of Jesus Christ, and stop judging people on what their beliefs are. We are all equal. There is only one person above any of us, and that is God, our master. I used to be just like many of the people are today, not sure of what to believe. I was lost, broken, not sure if there was a heaven, hell or if we truly had a God. But now I know that we do, indeed, have a loving and forgiving God. Heaven and hell do exist and depending upon what we choose with our own hearts is where we will spend our eternal life.

I can't imagine how people are going to feel the day that the trumpet sounds and Christ appears in the clouds. My heart breaks for the ones who don't believe in God and will be left behind. If you have children who are not of age to be accountable for their sins, they will be gone in the blink of an eye, just like all of the believers. And if you are not a believer and don't have Jesus in your heart, you will be separated from your children and family members. I just can't imagine what it will feel like for those parents when they realize their children are gone. You don't have to be in church to accept Jesus into your heart. You can be at home, the park, in the car, in the shower, wherever you want to be, because God is always with us. But you have to accept Jesus with your heart and not just your mouth and truly mean it.

It's hard to fathom as a human how the rapture will happen, how the dead in Christ will first rise then the believers next. I know I'm not going to die of an illness, car wreck, or any other way than the rapture because God told me, and He always keeps His promises. So I prayed and asked God to show me what it's going to look like and how the rapture will occur. He showed me in a vision, and I was floating up in the air with all the other believers. It was the most glorious vision I have seen. It's the most amazing way any of us can go. For the first time in our lives, we are going to be able to fly without the use of any planes but by the power of God. We're not going to die; we are just beginning to live.

One thing we must all understand is that God's time is His time and not ours. That's been the hardest lesson for me to learn, especially during writing this book. I've had to wait until the Lord was ready to reveal to me the pieces He wanted in the book and for Him to tell me when the book was complete. But during this entire process, God has been absolutely amazing and gentle with me when I wasn't quite where I needed to be. I just have to praise Him for His gentleness.

It's hard to sit back and wait sometimes for God to answer our prayers, but we can't be defiant and take matters into our own hands. The more we try to control things in our lives and the world, the more the devil succeeds in what he hopes to conquer. I have oftentimes wondered why things happen the way they do, whether it be the timing or the place.

One of my biggest complaints with my children is the amount of television they watch. While I was sick, they watched a lot of television since I was unable to take them to the park or be outside with them. Once I was healed, I realized that I had been using the television and other electronics to babysit my kids. At one time, both of my kids had televisions in their rooms, along with a Nintendo DS. Until one day, I decided to remove the televisions from both of their bedrooms so they would have to watch television with me and their dad. I found myself getting frustrated constantly with the fact that I couldn't get their attention. I prayed many times for God to help me with this situation.

Then one day, my son had the iPad that cost around five hundred dollars, and he dropped it and it shattered. He came to me and said, "Mom, you're going to be mad at me." But for some reason, I had great peace about it. I wasn't upset at all. And then the Holy Ghost revealed to me our children are so absorbed in electronics today and not learning about their heavenly Father. My children watched a lot of television and played video games, and not one of the games or shows did I see or hear them teach my children about God. The devil knew all along if he could find something that would keep the children occupied and that would give the parents a few minutes to have alone, he would be able to reach the innocent children.

Our kids have a job to do for the Lord, just like we do as adults. We have to be careful what we allow our children to watch. From the day we were born, God gave us a job, and we can't do it if were staying inside our homes absorbed with electronics. God wants and desires for us to go out and love and help others and not be absorbed with the worldly things. To be what God made us to be and use the gifts He blessed us with. Just because you don't have the job that you had envisioned doesn't mean God loves you any less. He has put you exactly where He needs you. God places us right where He wants us, but we have to listen and make sure it's not our flesh making the decision but God.

Many people don't believe that Jesus Christ will return and take all his believers to heaven, as it's spoken in Revelation, but this is another truth, and when this day comes, the ones who are left behind are going to be shocked. But will it be their fault or their teacher's fault? We will all be accountable for all our actions and the words we have spoken. It's one thing if we are speaking the truth and the people don't want to accept it, but it's something totally different if we are lying to the children of God.

After my lesson on the truth versus what people's flesh believes, I hit my knees and prayed because it was very confusing and overwhelming for me to know what to believe, with all the different books and beliefs people have. I told the Lord that night I would only look to one person for the truth and that was to Him, I know He's the only person I can trust to always tell me the truth and be there for me when I need Him. While I was sick, I would go to several doctors to seek treatment, but when it was all over, there was only one person who could save me and loved me enough to do so, and that was God.

The Bible is very complicated, and many people have taken the scriptures and allowed their minds to depict what they wanted them to read, and that is exactly what the devil wanted to happen all along. Satan has taken over our world today, because we have fallen away from God, because of things that happen in churches and because of the Word being taught wrong. I have had people tell me that because someone did something they were sent straight to hell. I have done things in my past that I have heard people say one goes to hell for. God forgave me, and He will forgive you, but you have to ask. We do not have the right to condemn anyone to hell, but we have the right to love and pray for them and teach them about the love Jesus has for each of us and how He died for us so we will be forgiven for our sins.

Our souls are like the stars in the sky. Some have a bright light that moves around the earth and shares God's glory while others have a dim light and never move around sharing God's works and wonders. Then there are those souls that are like a falling star. At one point, they had a bright light, but because of something that happened in their life, the light fell out. But we have to understand God is always with us. We need to not be ashamed to talk about God when we're out in public at the stores or with our friends. He is awesome and should be glorified during the entire day.

Now is the time for us to relight the light in our souls and do the work God has laid in our hearts. Go out and talk about His love for each of us and how He gave His only Son for us, and because of that, we all have the opportunity for an amazing everlasting life. But we have to accept God's Son and believe the true Gospel of Jesus Christ. That Jesus did die on the cross and is our redeemer. That Jesus did indeed leave the tomb and is in heaven with His father.

When you believe the true Gospel of Jesus Christ, that's when you know you have Jesus deep in your heart. To believe you can't analyze everything or expect to see it written on plain paper, it will come to you in your spirit and by faith. God is trying to relight the fire in people and wake them up for the events that are getting ready to happen, but we, as God's children, need to listen to what He is saying and wants us to do.

Our time here on earth is short, and we need to share with both the young and old generation the story of Jesus and the promises that were made to us in the Bible.

It's time to put our differences to the side and do what God is telling us to do and teach the truth out of His book and not what our flesh believes. It doesn't matter what we think what matters is the truth. Our money, fancy homes, cars, or materialistic things will not get us into heaven; in fact, they might prevent you from making it to heaven. If we're so absorbed in the world and the things in it, how are we doing what God called us to do? Our reward is not here but in heaven; we just need to listen and do what our heavenly Father asks of us. People need to hear the truth or they will never change. Everything will stay the same and get worse as time goes by. We all like to hear what makes us feel good, but we need to hear and know the truth. Is it difficult sometimes?

Yes, but it will be easier to hear it now than when Christ comes and you're left behind.

No matter what religion we are, we are all going to face the day of judgment. "For we must all appear before the judgment seat of Christ, that each one may receive what is due him for the things done while in the body, whether good or bad" (2 Corinthians 5:10, NIV). We should all be seeking God in these days. We should stop the worldly things that consume our lives for the love that we have for Jesus. What we see and know today could be over tomorrow, so the question to ask yourself is this: is going shopping, having your nails done, or attending a ball game more important to you than making sure you're right with God for when Christ comes for us?

We live in a very fast-paced world today, and it's hard to find time to even rest, but we need to take time to pray and seek God and know that God will give us the time we need. We should all be as hungry for the Word of God as the people in South America. They will walk miles to listen to a minister preach, but the United States of America, for some reason, has let the devil take over the country, homes, schools, and government. We have taken God out of every part of our lives where He used to dwell. I believe if people really knew how soon Christ was coming they would be filling the church buildings up and be receiving Jesus into their hearts. "If my people, who are called by my name, will humble themselves and pray and seek my face and turn from their wicked ways, then will I hear from heaven and forgive their sin and will heal their land" (2 Chronicles 7:14, NIV).

Tribulation is going to be a time of horror. On the rock, it shows the seals of what was promised to us, and what will happen during this time. It is time we rise up and stand up for God, Jesus, and the Holy Ghost. We would not be here today if it wasn't for God and Jesus Christ. Because of Jesus dying on the cross, we have all been forgiven for our sins. We just have to accept Jesus into our hearts. We have a loving and forgiving God who wants nothing more than for all His children to wake up and come home on the day that Christ comes to get us. You must be born again to enter the Kingdom of God.

The second hardest lesson I have had to learn during the time of writing this book was to walk in faith and to believe in what we feel and know in our spirit although we can't physically touch it. God is wanting us all to step out in faith and believe and trust in what we have been taught for all these years that He is, indeed, a real, loving, and forgiving God before His Son, Jesus Christ, comes back to get all of God's children who believe in Him.

The title of this book, *God's Gift*, was given to me from God when I was writing the first part. I knew that the gift God had given me was my salvation and a second chance in life. But while writing the second half of the book, the Lord revealed to me the second half of the title, *The Rock, which is God's gift to America.* The Rock is Jesus Christ, our salvation. Jesus died on the cross and was raised from the dead on the third day so each and every one of us could have the free gift of salvation and everlasting life. Jesus is alive and is sitting with His Father on the right-hand side of the throne, waiting for His commandment to come and get the body of the church who believe in Him.

We all must understand there is only one God, the creator of our universe. Our human minds can't even begin to imagine the power our God has, but to think about it is absolutely amazing. As children of God, our job is to walk by faith, not by sight. I strongly encourage every person who does not know Jesus Christ as their Lord and Savior to read the prayer below. If you do know Jesus Christ as your Lord and Savior and want to be baptized by the Holy Ghost, I have also written that prayer down below.

God is amazing, and Jesus Christ made the sacrifice for us so we could experience the free gift of salvation and the Holy Spirit. God loves each and every one of us, and He wants all His children to come home to heaven when His son, Jesus Christ, returns to get us. But for those who don't listen, they are going to witness a time they never thought could or would happen. It doesn't matter if you've been a Bible scholar for fifty years, a church leader, or anything else. When Christ returns, all that's going to matter is that you know that Jesus Christ is your Lord and Savior and that we only have one God.

> After reading Sister Anita's book, if you are a sinner and would like to be saved, may we help you? I would like to lead you in the sinner's prayer. Father, I know that I am a sinner and have done wrong. I would like to repent. I ask you to save me in the precious name of your Son, Jesus Christ, who died on the cross, shedding

His blood that I could be saved. I am believing in my heart and confessing my sins with my mouth. I thank you for saving me. Please read: Romans 10:9, 1 John 1:9, and Acts 2:21 (NIV).

—Written by Pastor J. W. Copeland

You are now saved and on your way to the kingdom of God! You are a Christian, a child of the Almighty God. You are saved and freed from all your sins. The Word also says, "If ye then, being evil, know how to give good gifts unto your children: how much more shall your heavenly Father give the Holy Spirit to them that ask Him?" (Luke 11:13, NIV). Father, I'm also asking you to fill me with the Holy Spirit. Holy Spirit, rise up within me as I praise God. I fully expect to speak with other tongues as You give me utterance (Acts 2:4, NIV).

Begin to praise God for saving you and filling you with the Holy Spirit. Let Him know how much you love Him. Speak the words and syllables you receive, not in your own language but in the language that God has given to you by the Holy Spirit. Ask the Holy Spirit to guide and teach you as you speak in your new language. Praise and worship God in your new heavenly language and always tell God, Jesus Christ, and the Holy Spirit, "I love you, and thank you."

If you want someone to pray the prayers with you, I have placed contact information in the back, and we would be happy to lead you to the Lord and talk to you. I encourage you to spend time in prayer seeking God and ask Him to lead you and your family to a church where the true Gospel is taught. I found it very important, and still do today, to spend time in church learning from the people of God. It was a challenge at first, but God led me to different churches in the area that I live in. I have been truly blessed by the preachers whom God has led me to, to teach me and guide me in the direction I'm at today. Always remember there is only one person who knows the absolute truth of when Christ is going to return, how it's going to happen, and what the people who are left behind are going to experience, and that's God—no one else.

While writing this book, I asked the Lord to show me what people were going to experience during tribulation, and one night, in a dream, He showed me. What I saw was absolutely horrific. In my dream, I remembered the Lord was right beside me, and I yelled out a curse word, and automatically I started repenting. But the Lord said, "It's okay. People think they know what it's going to be like, but it's not what they have imagined." It was absolutely terrifying what the Lord revealed to me that night in my dream.

I pray daily for God to search the hearts of my family, friends, and of the people in America who are lost. No one has to go through what's going to happen. God has given each of us a choice: either continue to live in sin and not accept His son, Jesus Christ, as Lord and Savior and be left behind, or accept His son and go to the most glorious place we will ever know, heaven.

May God bless each and every person who reads this book. I pray that God will protect you from all evil and from being deceived, that He will give you boldness to stand up for what is right so you will go out and preach the powerful Gospel of Jesus Christ and save souls. And that He will bless you with peace and joy until the day that Christ returns. This book was written from my heart to yours. I love each and every one of you, and I pray you have been touched with the message the Lord has asked me to deliver to His children in America and around the world.

Love,
Anita J. Shipman
God's Lights of Life Ministry
P.O. Box 454
Wagoner, Oklahoma 74477
ashipman31@me.com

Picture that shows the side profile face.
1 Thessalonians 4:16 (NIV).

Picture that shows the seal of the body.
Thessalonians 4:14(NIV)

Picture of the Opposum which symbolizes how
the church will be asleep in the final days.

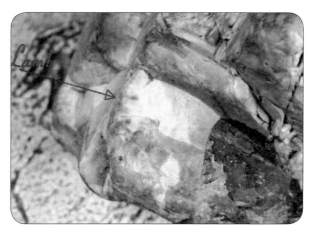

Picture of the Lamb located on the side of the rock.

Picture of the cow

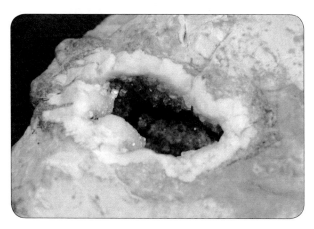

Picture of the tomb located on the bottom of the rock.

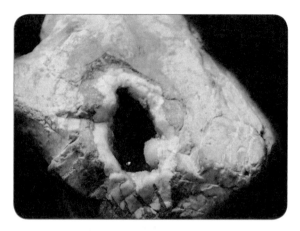

Silhouette of Jesus walking out of the tomb. Luke 24:1-6(NIV)

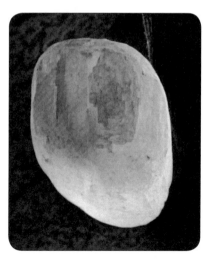

Picture of the white rock that fits over the tomb,
that shows Jesus's face on the right side.

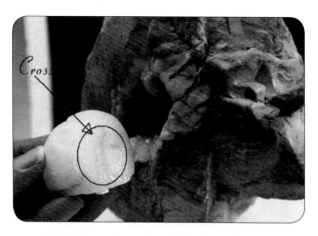

Side of the white rock which shows the cross.

Pictures of the four horses of tribulation
found in the book of Revelation.

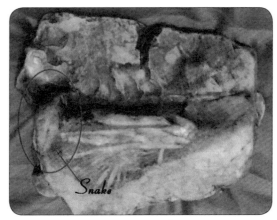

Picture of the snake located on the rock which symbolizes satan.

Picture of the rock when held upside down
and the white rock over the tomb.

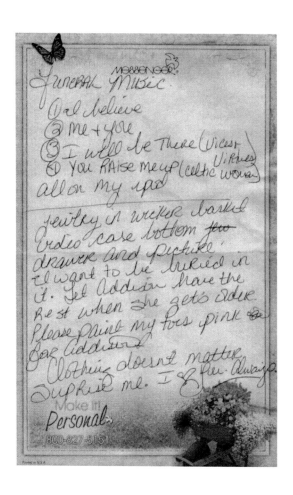

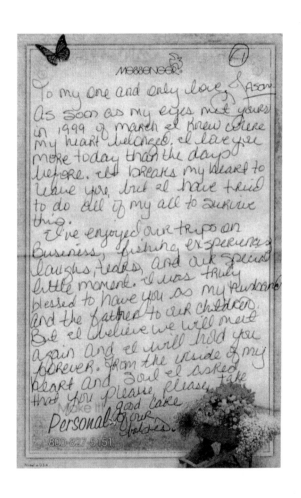

To my one and only love, Jason.
As soon as my eyes met yours
in 1999 of March I knew where
my heart belonged. I love you
more today than the days
before. It breaks my heart to
leave you, but I have tried
to do all of my all to survive
this.
I've enjoyed our trips on
Business, fishing experiences,
laughs, tears, and our special
little moments. I was truly
blessed to have you as my husband,
and the father to our children.
But I believe we will meet
again and I will hold you
forever. From the inside of my
heart and soul I asked
that you please please, take
good care

they are my world, you 3 complete me. I want you to be happy, and even Remarry, but please protect our children, cause I will protect you 3 from above day & night. I love you so much. Please tell Ryan & Addison I love them every night. I would like for you to be buried next to me even if you do Remarry. You know you have always completed me! thank you for all of your love and support through the years. Our love hasn't died just because I did. Believe that I will always be with you. you've been a great husband + your a great dad and never forget that. Going to Rest for now. more to come. I love you sexy

4-26-12.

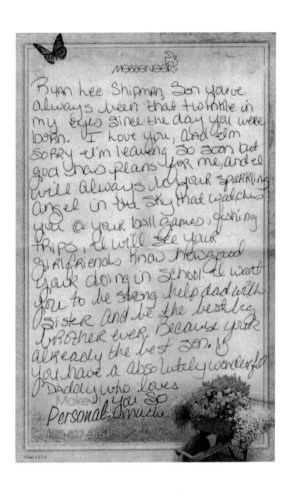

Ryan Lee Shipman, Son you've always been that twinkle in my eyes since the day you were born. I love you, and I'm sorry I'm leaving so soon but god has plans for me, and I will always be your sparkling angel in the sky that watches you @ your ball games, fishing trips, I will see your girlfriends know how good your doing in school. I want you to be strong help dad with sister and be the best big brother ever. Because your already the best son. You have a absolutely wonderful Daddy who loves you so much.

If you ever need anything
Please just talk to him.
You make me so proud to
be your mother, and know I
will always be your mom.
And Sparkling Angel. But
if your dad meets another
girl please be nice nice!!.
I know your going to be hurt
when I leave, but just hang
on to the memories we made and
shared with each other, treasure
them and pictures and know I'm
with you at all times. The pain
will heal in a matter of time
son, your very smart, and
handsome. So please promise
me you will work hard in school.
help dadely with sister. This
world we live in is hard but
you can do it just take it by
the horns and be who you
want to be and who god

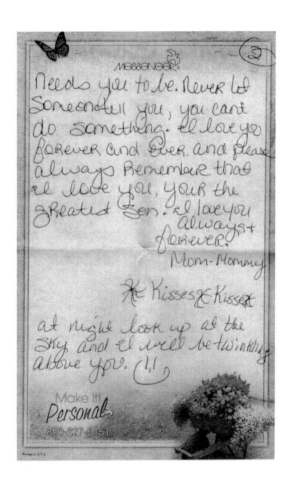

needs you to be. never let someone tell you, you cant do something. I love you forever and ever. and please always Remember that I love you, your the greatest son. I love you always + forever. Mom-Mommy

Kisses Kisses

at night look up at the sky and I will be twinkling above you.

Addison Nicole, not sure you will understand what is happening, but mommy has gone to be your sparkling angel in the sky. You + I are so much alike, your a sweet, sweet, ambitous young girl. Whatever you decide to do in life please be sure your Happy. alts very important. Always listen to Daddy. he knows what is right- The hardest thing I will ever do is leaving you, daddy and Bubba behind but it's my time, but that doesn't mean I don't love you.

A few simple Rules for later on
in your life 1. Never have sex, just
because they want to.
2. Always tell daddy where
you are.
3. If you ever have girl question
you can always ask Nana or
Aunt Jen.
And never forget I will loe
you to the moon and back.
And I cant wait to see how
you grow from above while I'm
your Sparkling Angel. I love
You Sister & always will.
                    Love always
                        Mommy
                            4-26-12